Meet

Martin Luther King Jr.

Meet
Martin Luther King Jr.

by Johnny Ray Moore

Illustrated by Amy Wummer

ideals children's books™

Nashville, Tennessee

ISBN 0-8249-5486-6

Published by Ideals Children's Books
An imprint of Ideals Publications
A division of Guideposts
535 Metroplex Drive, Suite 250
Nashville, Tennessee 37211
www.idealsbooks.com

Film separations by Precision Color Graphics, Franklin, Wisconsin

Printed and bound in Mexico by RR Donnelley

Library of Congress Cataloging-in-Publication data on file

10 9 8 7 6 5 4 3 2

To my wife, Jackie, and our daughters,
Jenell, Jyrita, and Jamica.

When the history books are written, someone
will say there lived black people who had the
courage to stand up for their rights.

—Martin Luther King Jr.

Go on home,

Martin," said the woman at the door. "**My boys can't play with you anymore.**"

Five-year-old Martin Luther King Jr. turned away from the house and raced down the street.

When Martin got to his own house, his mother said, "**Son, tell me what happened.**"

Martin told his mother about the white woman who

wouldn't let her two boys play with him anymore.

"I thought we were friends," Martin said.

Martin's mother explained that states in the southern part of the country had Jim Crow laws that said black people and white people must stay apart. Black children could not go to school with white children.

Black people could not eat in restaurants with white people. Blacks could not drink from the same water fountains as whites.

"That's not fair," said Martin.
"That's the way it is," said his mother.
Martin never forgot those two white boys and their mother. He would find a way for all people to live and play together.

Martin was born in Atlanta, Georgia, on January 15, 1929. He was named for his father, Martin Luther King Sr., who was minister of the Ebenezer Baptist Church. Every Sunday morning, Martin, his older sister, Christine, and his younger brother, Alfred, went to church and listened to their father preach.

Martin liked his father's sermons, and he saw that many people respected his father. Martin wondered if he would be a preacher, just like his dad.

Martin loved to read. His mother, Alberta, had

been a schoolteacher. Perhaps she helped him find

books about great black people. Stories about

former slave Frederick Douglass, who had

escaped to freedom and then helped other

slaves, showed Martin how a person can change

the lives of others. Stories about Booker T.

Washington, who founded the first college

for blacks, showed him how important

education can be. And stories

about George Washington Carver, who

developed many uses for the peanut,

showed Martin that imagination can

change the world.

Martin never forgot these stories. He too had

courage and imagination. And he wanted the best

education he could get.

Martin made good grades in school and skipped the ninth and twelfth grades. His scores on the college exams were so good that he didn't have to finish high school. Martin was only fifteen years old when he entered Morehouse College in Atlanta.

After graduation, Martin went to Chester, Pennsylvania, and enrolled in Crozier Theological Seminary. He had decided to become a preacher like his father.

Then Martin heard about a man in India named Mahatma Gandhi.

Gandhi led his followers in peaceful marches against the Indian

government. Gandhi made a better life for his people.

Martin still had not forgotten the white woman who would not let her

sons play with him. He wondered if his world could be changed through

peaceful marches like Gandhi's. Martin began to imagine a world where

blacks and whites lived together in peace and love.

When Martin graduated from Crozier, he won an award of money to

continue his education. He went to Boston University. In Boston, Martin

met and fell in love with Coretta Scott, who was studying music. Martin

and Coretta were married in 1953. They had four children: Yolanda

Denise, Dexter Scott, Bernie Albertine, and Martin Luther King III.

Martin finished his studies at
Boston University. Now he was Dr.
Martin Luther King Jr. and he began
to look for a job where he could help
his people. In 1954, the Dexter
Avenue Baptist Church in
Montgomery, Alabama, called Martin
to be their pastor. He accepted, and
he and Coretta moved to Alabama.

Alabama had Jim Crow laws just like Atlanta. Black children did not
go to school with white children. Blacks rode in the backs of the buses.
One day in December 1955, a woman named Rosa Parks boarded the bus
and sat down. The bus driver told her to give up her seat to a white man
who was left standing. When Rosa said no, the police arrested her.

Martin told all blacks in Montgomery, **"Do not ride the buses to work. Walk or take a taxi."** For the next year, the buses in Montgomery were empty.

The white people of Montgomery were angry. Blacks were angry too. Some gathered on Martin's lawn. They were ready to fight for their rights, but Martin said **"no fighting."** He told them it takes more courage to protest peacefully.

Then the United States Supreme Court said that no city could make black people sit in the back of the bus and no bus driver could order black people to give up their seats. Martin and Rosa and the black people of Montgomery could sit on the bus anywhere they wanted.

But blacks still could not go to school with whites. And they could not vote. Martin knew that these laws must also be changed. Martin asked people to come to Washington, D.C., and show the world that blacks should be allowed to vote.

On August 28, 1963, more than 250,000 people listened as Martin spoke to them. He said, **"I have a dream . . . that someday my four little children will not be judged by the color of their skin. . . ."**

Back in Alabama, Martin wanted to help blacks register to vote. He called for a march from the town of Selma to Montgomery, the capital of Alabama, fifty-four miles away.

On the morning of March 21, 1965, 3,000 people started marching. They walked all day. At night, they slept on the ground.

After five days, Martin led the marchers into Montgomery. And by the end of the summer, 9,000 people had registered to vote.

Martin knew there were more people to help. In April 1968, he went to Memphis, Tennessee, to lead garbage collectors in a march for better pay. But while he stood on the balcony of his motel, James Earl Ray shot Martin.

After Martin's death, the Congress of the United States

made Martin's birthday, January 15, a national holiday.

Martin loved helping people. He showed the world that it took courage to stand up for equality and for freedom. But mostly, Martin taught us all how to love each other and how to live in peace.